PRACTICE

FINISH TRACING THE LETTERS OF EACH ROW
AS PROVIDED BY THE EXAMPLES!

FINISH TRACING THE LETTERS OF EACH ROW
AS PROVIDED BY THE EXAMPLES!

PRACTICE

FINISH TRACING THE LETTERS OF EACH ROW
AS PROVIDED BY THE EXAMPLES!

PRACTICE

FINISH TRACING THE LETTERS OF EACH ROW
AS PROVIDED BY THE EXAMPLES!

FINISH TRACING THE LETTERS OF EACH ROW
AS PROVIDED BY THE EXAMPLES!

FINISH TRACING THE LETTERS OF EACH ROW
AS PROVIDED BY THE EXAMPLES!

FINISH TRACING THE LETTERS OF EACH ROW
AS PROVIDED BY THE EXAMPLES!

PRACTICE

FINISH TRACING THE LETTERS OF EACH ROW
AS PROVIDED BY THE EXAMPLES!

PRACTICE

FINISH TRACING THE LETTERS OF EACH ROW
AS PROVIDED BY THE EXAMPLES!

PRACTICE

FINISH TRACING THE LETTERS OF EACH ROW
AS PROVIDED BY THE EXAMPLES!

PRACTICE

PRACTICE

FINISH TRACING THE LETTERS OF EACH ROW
AS PROVIDED BY THE EXAMPLES!

PRACTICE

FINISH TRACING THE LETTERS OF EACH ROW AS PROVIDED BY THE EXAMPLES!

PRACTICE

FINISH TRACING THE LETTERS OF EACH ROW
AS PROVIDED BY THE EXAMPLES!

PRACTICE

FINISH TRACING THE LETTERS OF EACH ROW
AS PROVIDED BY THE EXAMPLES!

PRACTICE

PRACTICE

PRACTICE

FINISH TRACING THE LETTERS OF EACH ROW
AS PROVIDED BY THE EXAMPLES!

PRACTICE

FINISH TRACING THE LETTERS OF EACH ROW
AS PROVIDED BY THE EXAMPLES!

PRACTICE

FINISH TRACING THE LETTERS OF EACH ROW
AS PROVIDED BY THE EXAMPLES!

PRACTICE

FINISH TRACING THE LETTERS OF EACH ROW
AS PROVIDED BY THE EXAMPLES!

PRACTICE

FINISH TRACING THE LETTERS OF EACH ROW
AS PROVIDED BY THE EXAMPLES!

PRACTICE

FINISH TRACING THE LETTERS OF EACH ROW
AS PROVIDED BY THE EXAMPLES!

PRACTICE

FINISH TRACING THE LETTERS OF EACH ROW
AS PROVIDED BY THE EXAMPLES!

PRACTICE

FINISH TRACING THE LETTERS OF EACH ROW
AS PROVIDED BY THE EXAMPLES!

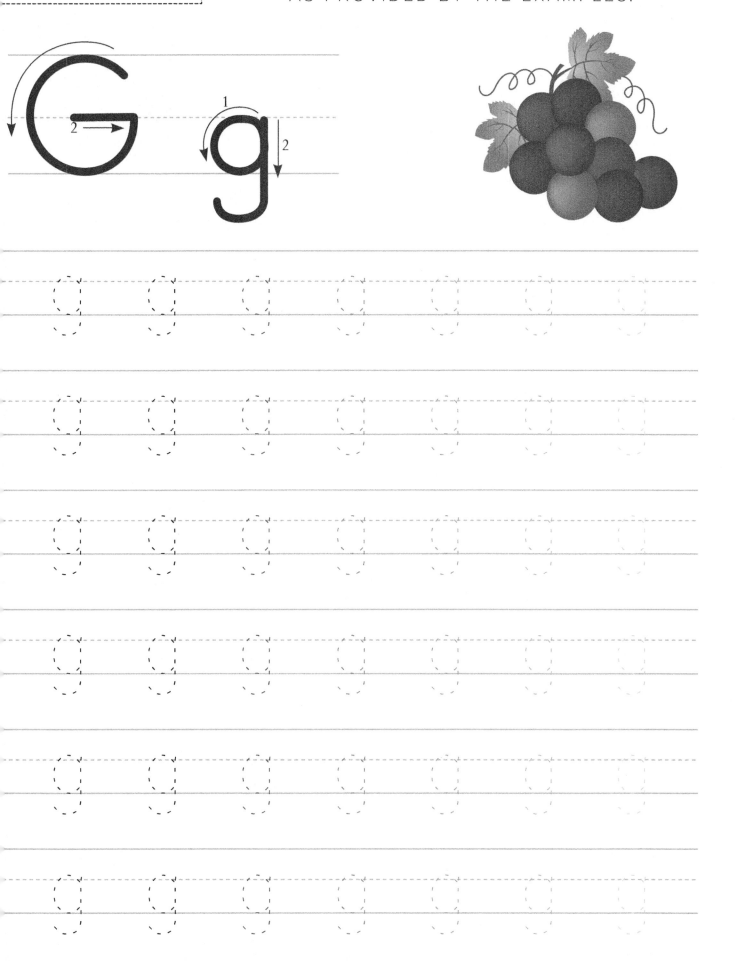

PRACTICE

FINISH TRACING THE LETTERS OF EACH ROW
AS PROVIDED BY THE EXAMPLES!

PRACTICE

FINISH TRACING THE LETTERS OF EACH ROW
AS PROVIDED BY THE EXAMPLES!

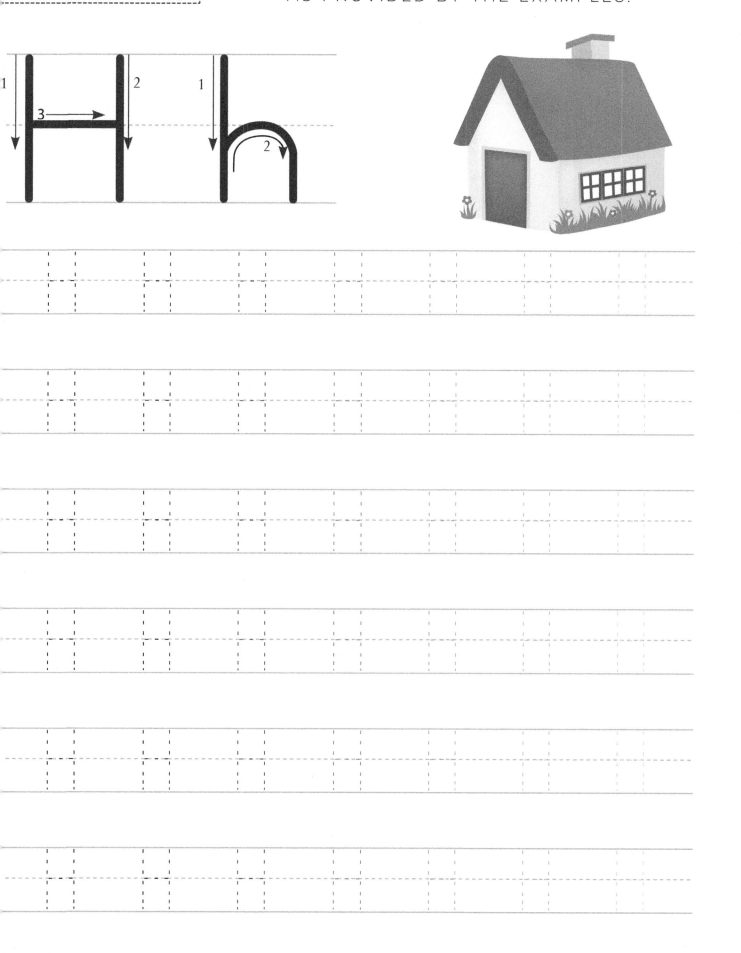

PRACTICE

FINISH TRACING THE LETTERS OF EACH ROW
AS PROVIDED BY THE EXAMPLES!

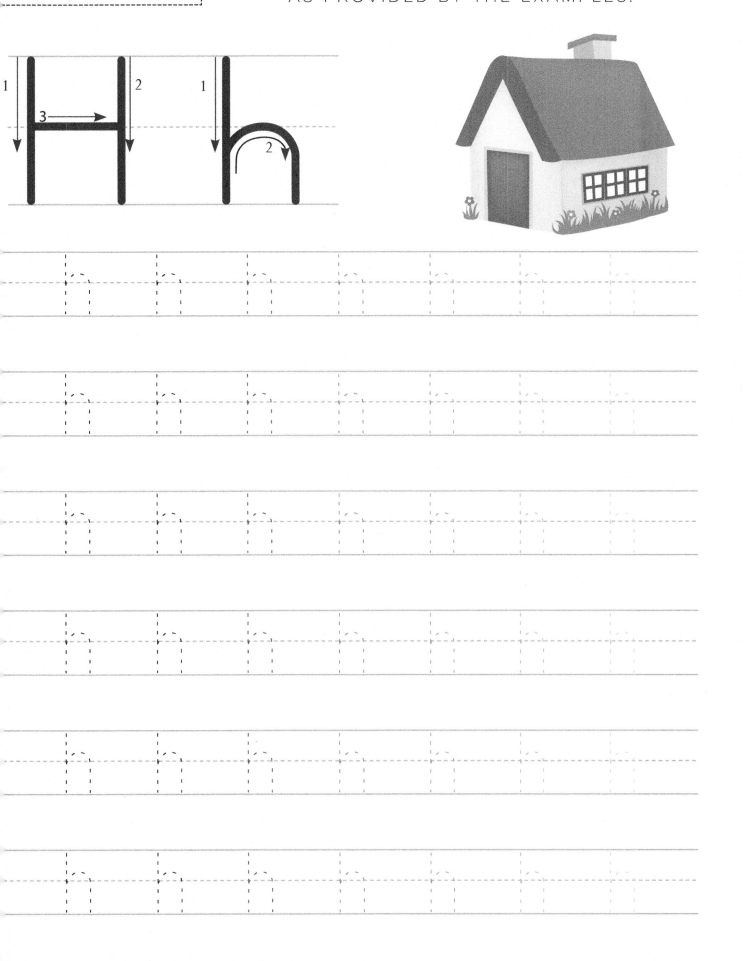

PRACTICE

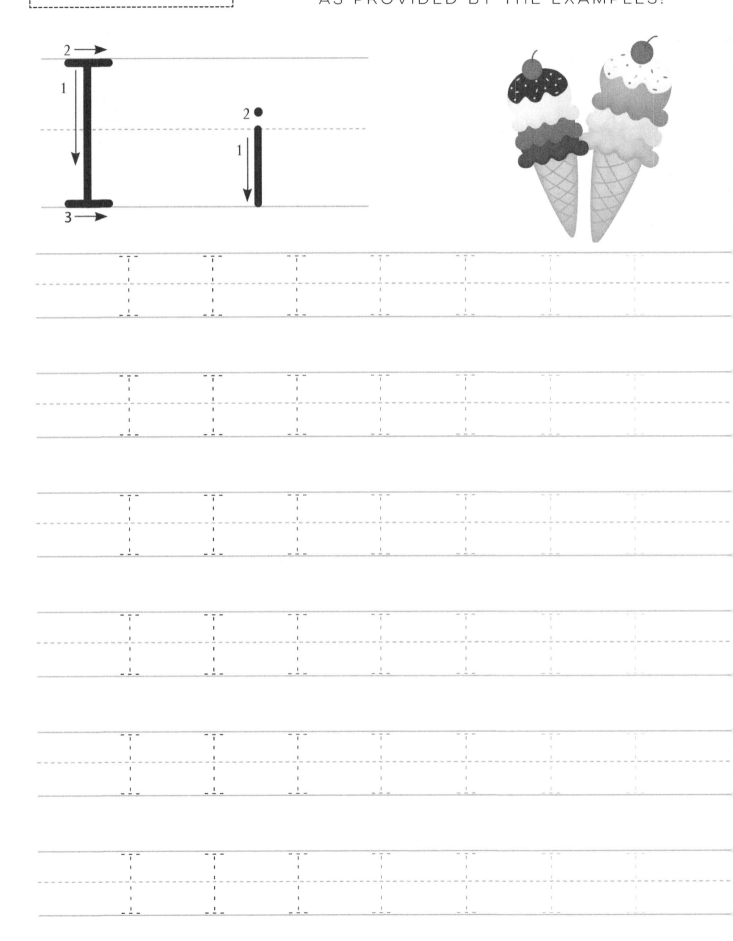

PRACTICE

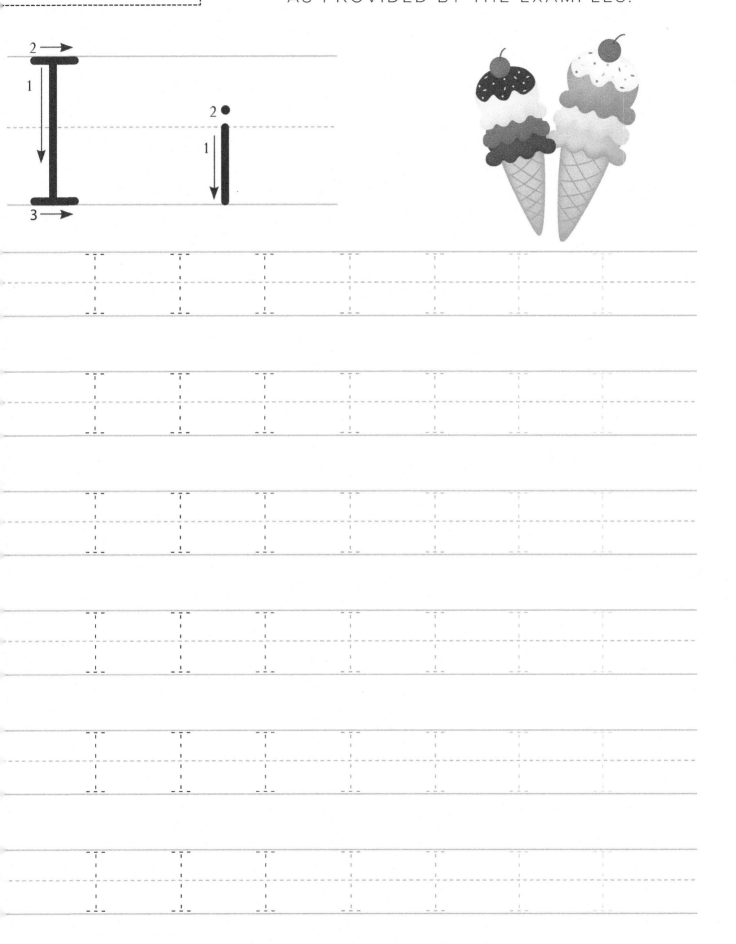

PRACTICE

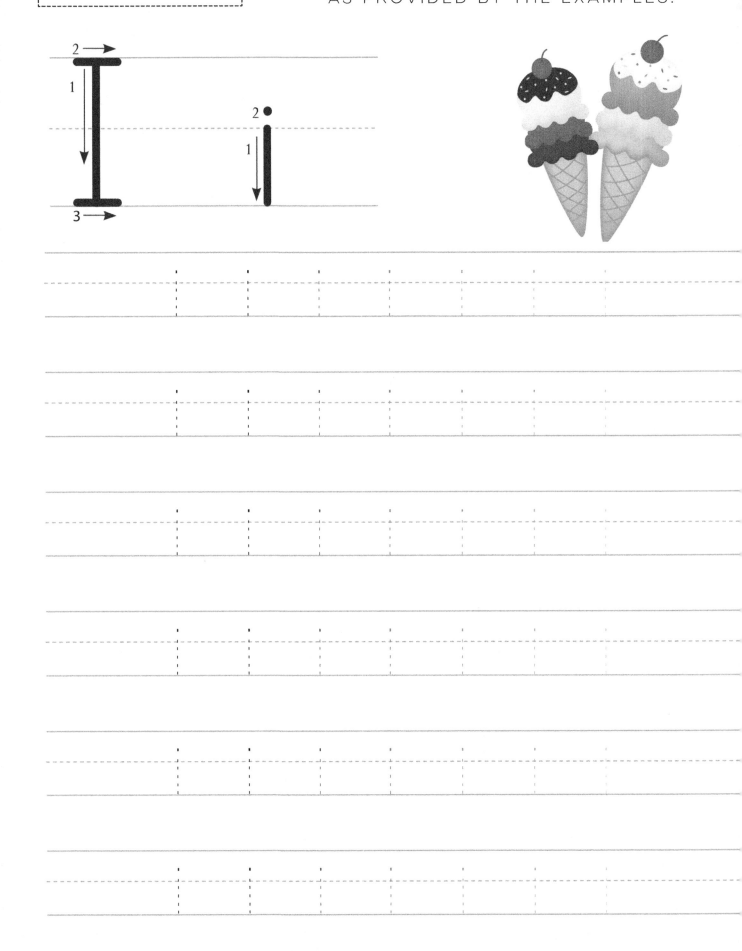

PRACTICE

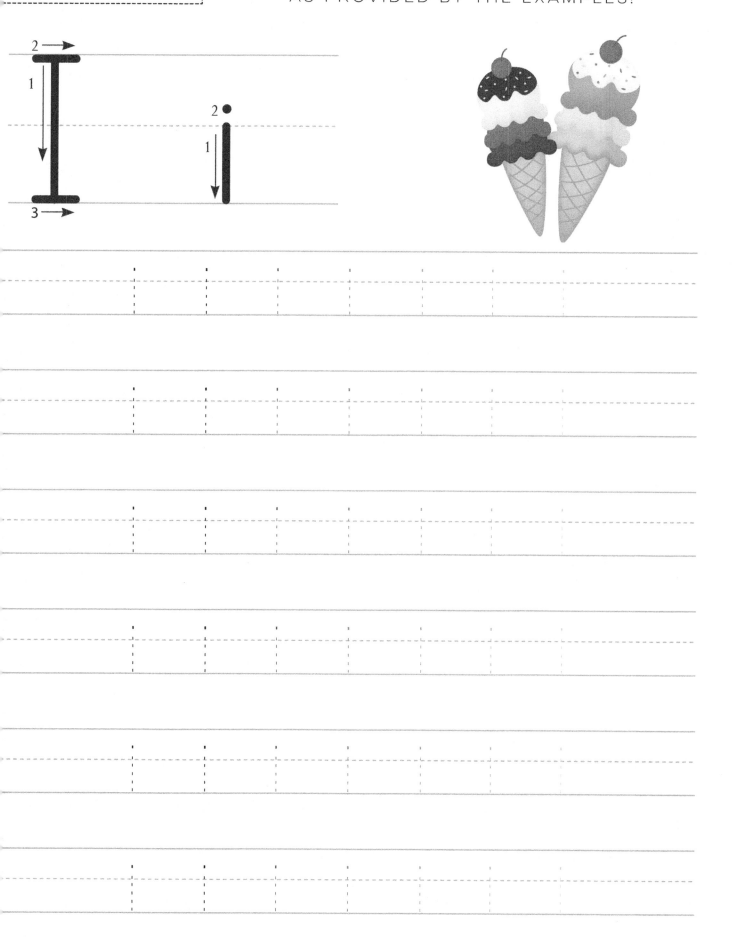

PRACTICE

FINISH TRACING THE LETTERS OF EACH ROW
AS PROVIDED BY THE EXAMPLES!

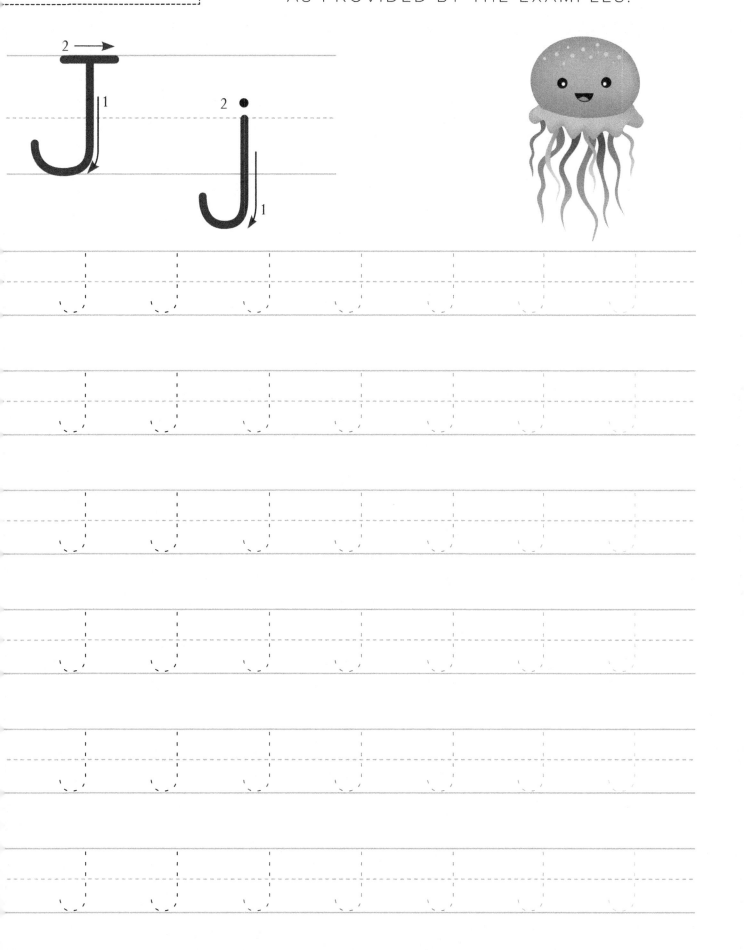

PRACTICE

FINISH TRACING THE LETTERS OF EACH ROW
AS PROVIDED BY THE EXAMPLES!

PRACTICE

FINISH TRACING THE LETTERS OF EACH ROW
AS PROVIDED BY THE EXAMPLES!

FINISH TRACING THE LETTERS OF EACH ROW
AS PROVIDED BY THE EXAMPLES!

PRACTICE

FINISH TRACING THE LETTERS OF EACH ROW
AS PROVIDED BY THE EXAMPLES!

PRACTICE

FINISH TRACING THE LETTERS OF EACH ROW
AS PROVIDED BY THE EXAMPLES!

FINISH TRACING THE LETTERS OF EACH ROW
AS PROVIDED BY THE EXAMPLES!

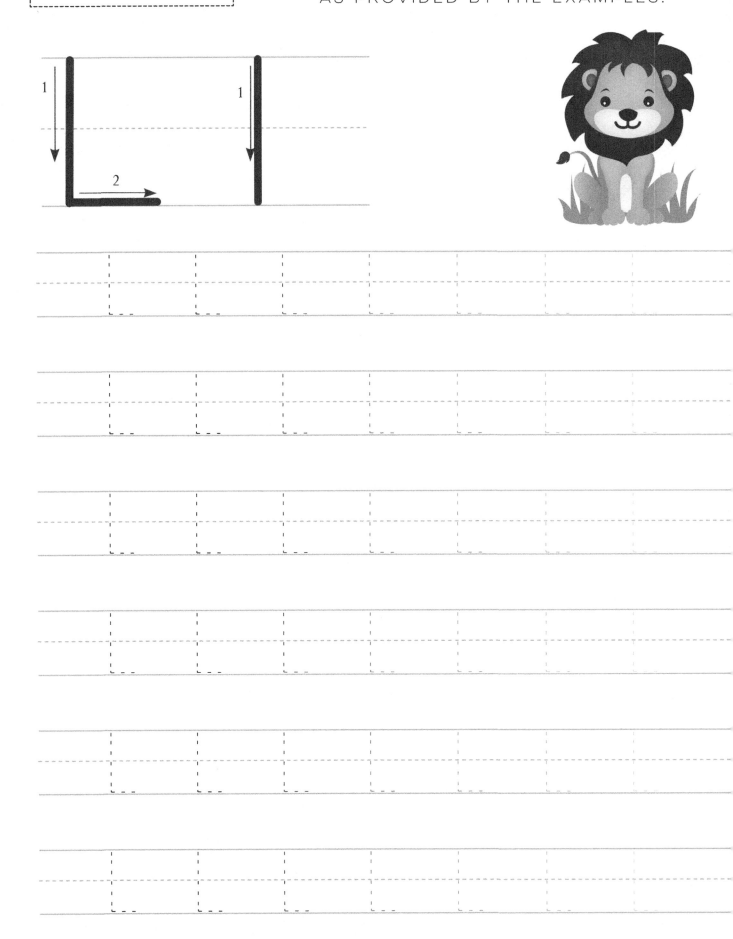

PRACTICE

FINISH TRACING THE LETTERS OF EACH ROW
AS PROVIDED BY THE EXAMPLES!

PRACTICE

FINISH TRACING THE LETTERS OF EACH ROW
AS PROVIDED BY THE EXAMPLES!

PRACTICE

FINISH TRACING THE LETTERS OF EACH ROW
AS PROVIDED BY THE EXAMPLES!

FINISH TRACING THE LETTERS OF EACH ROW
AS PROVIDED BY THE EXAMPLES!

PRACTICE

FINISH TRACING THE LETTERS OF EACH ROW
AS PROVIDED BY THE EXAMPLES!

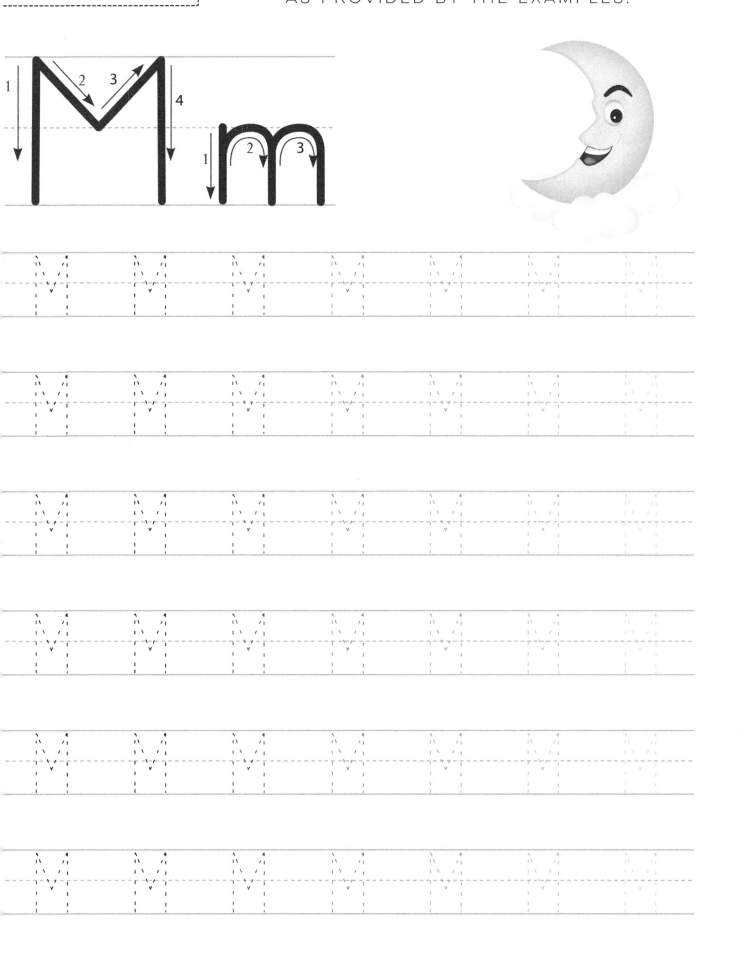

PRACTICE

FINISH TRACING THE LETTERS OF EACH ROW
AS PROVIDED BY THE EXAMPLES!

PRACTICE

FINISH TRACING THE LETTERS OF EACH ROW
AS PROVIDED BY THE EXAMPLES!

PRACTICE

PRACTICE

FINISH TRACING THE LETTERS OF EACH ROW
AS PROVIDED BY THE EXAMPLES!

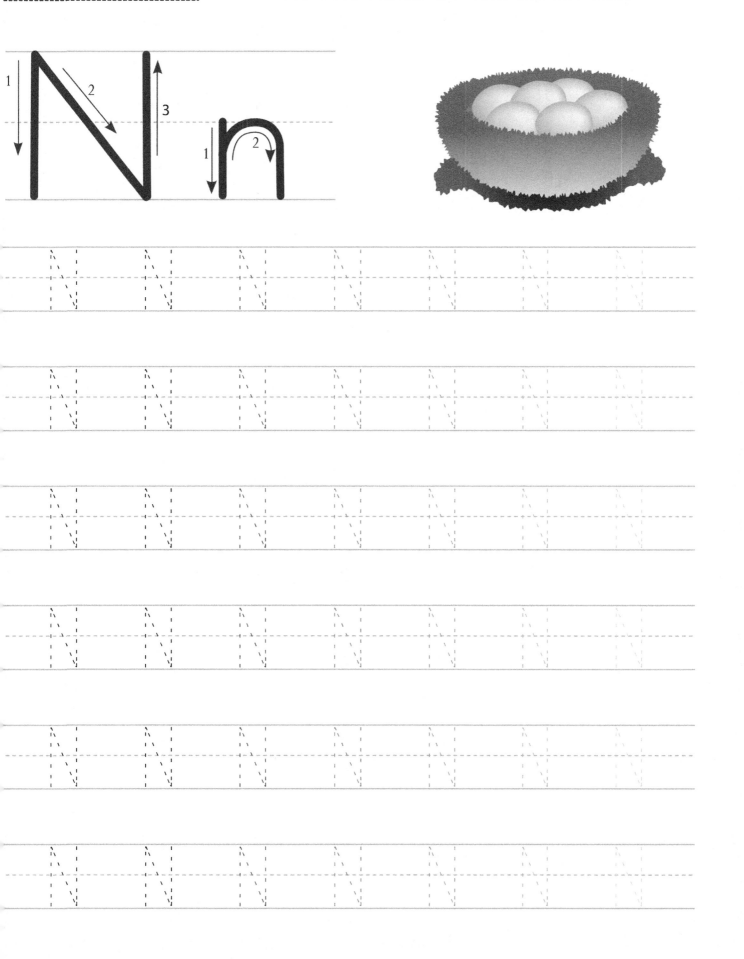

PRACTICE

FINISH TRACING THE LETTERS OF EACH ROW
AS PROVIDED BY THE EXAMPLES!

PRACTICE

FINISH TRACING THE LETTERS OF EACH ROW
AS PROVIDED BY THE EXAMPLES!

PRACTICE

FINISH TRACING THE LETTERS OF EACH ROW
AS PROVIDED BY THE EXAMPLES!

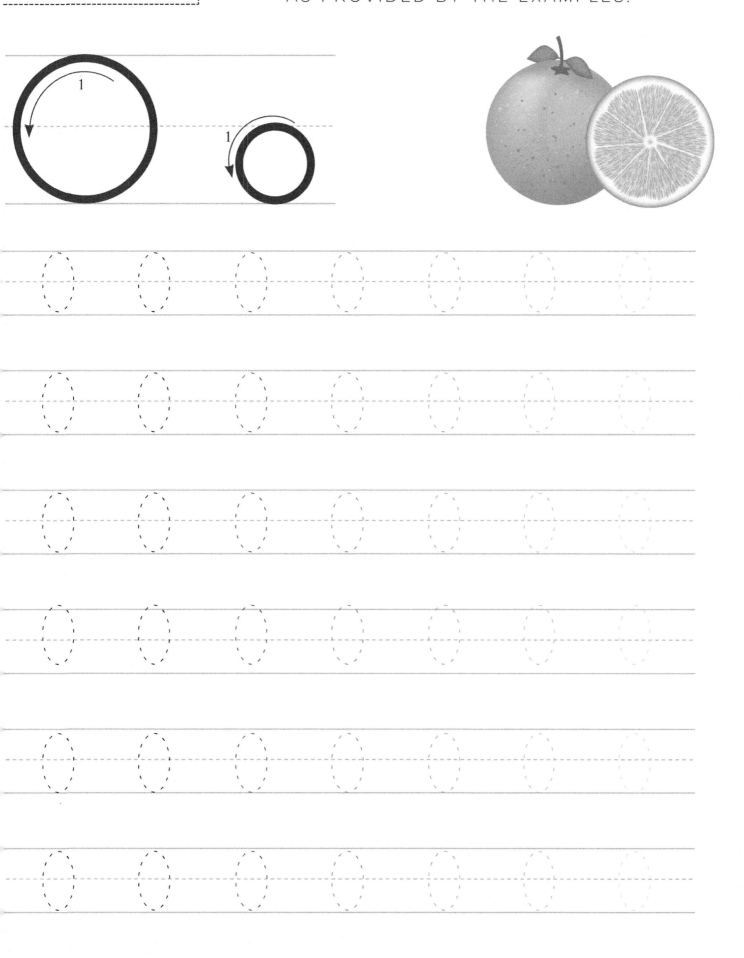

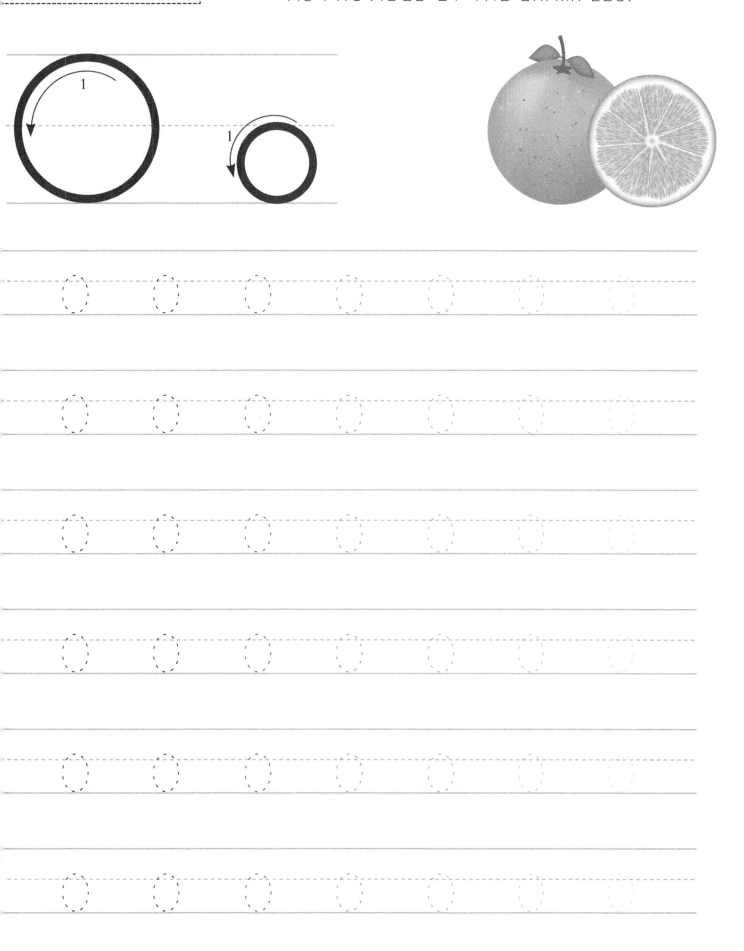

PRACTICE

FINISH TRACING THE LETTERS OF EACH ROW
AS PROVIDED BY THE EXAMPLES!

FINISH TRACING THE LETTERS OF EACH ROW
AS PROVIDED BY THE EXAMPLES!

FINISH TRACING THE LETTERS OF EACH ROW
AS PROVIDED BY THE EXAMPLES!

PRACTICE

FINISH TRACING THE LETTERS OF EACH ROW
AS PROVIDED BY THE EXAMPLES!

FINISH TRACING THE LETTERS OF EACH ROW
AS PROVIDED BY THE EXAMPLES!

PRACTICE

PRACTICE

PRACTICE

FINISH TRACING THE LETTERS OF EACH ROW
AS PROVIDED BY THE EXAMPLES!

PRACTICE

FINISH TRACING THE LETTERS OF EACH ROW
AS PROVIDED BY THE EXAMPLES!

PRACTICE

FINISH TRACING THE LETTERS OF EACH ROW
AS PROVIDED BY THE EXAMPLES!

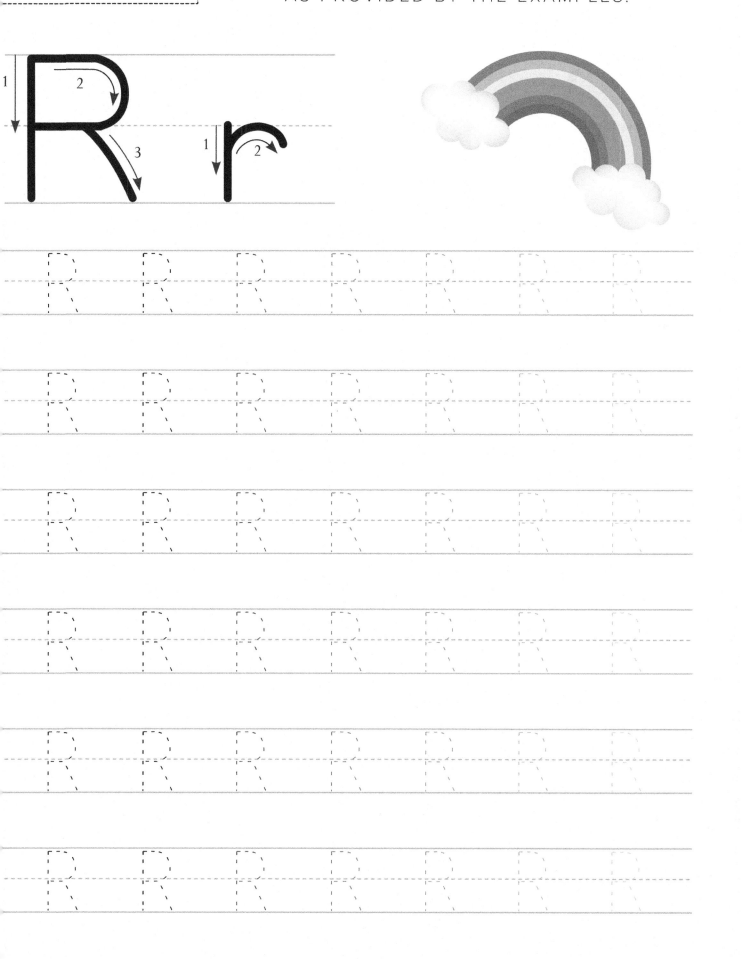

PRACTICE

FINISH TRACING THE LETTERS OF EACH ROW
AS PROVIDED BY THE EXAMPLES!

FINISH TRACING THE LETTERS OF EACH ROW
AS PROVIDED BY THE EXAMPLES!

PRACTICE

FINISH TRACING THE LETTERS OF EACH ROW
AS PROVIDED BY THE EXAMPLES!

PRACTICE

FINISH TRACING THE LETTERS OF EACH ROW
AS PROVIDED BY THE EXAMPLES!

PRACTICE

FINISH TRACING THE LETTERS OF EACH ROW
AS PROVIDED BY THE EXAMPLES!

PRACTICE

FINISH TRACING THE LETTERS OF EACH ROW
AS PROVIDED BY THE EXAMPLES!

PRACTICE

FINISH TRACING THE LETTERS OF EACH ROW
AS PROVIDED BY THE EXAMPLES!

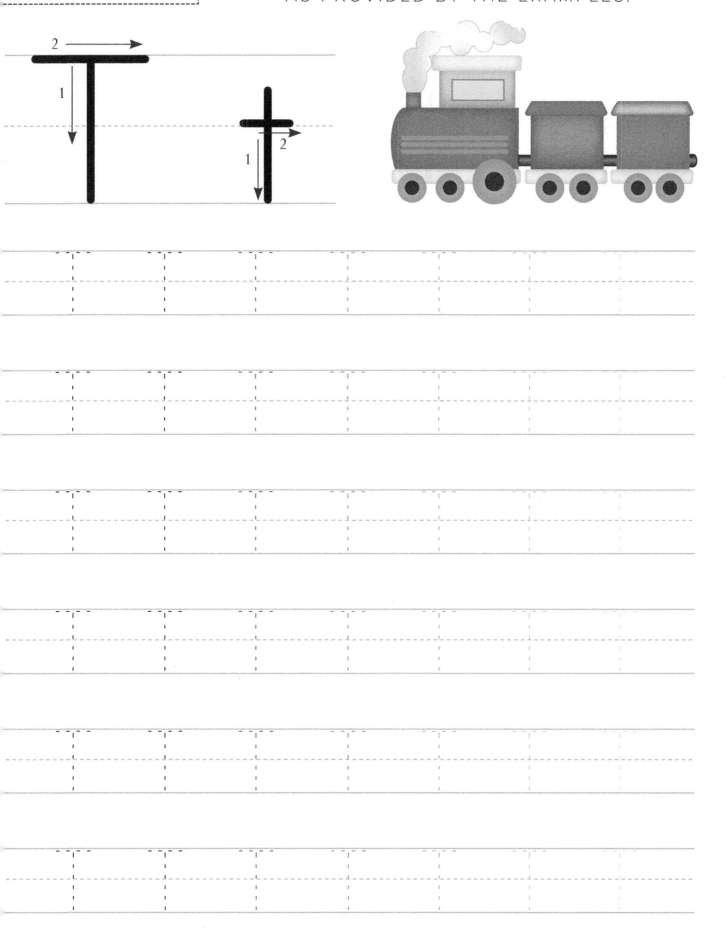

PRACTICE

FINISH TRACING THE LETTERS OF EACH ROW AS PROVIDED BY THE EXAMPLES!

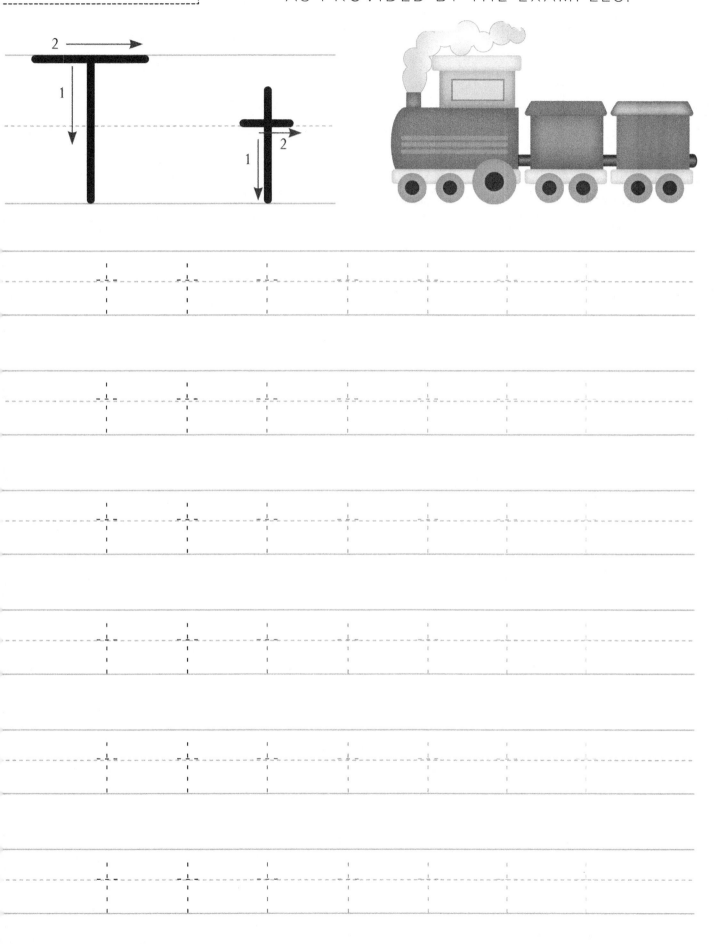

PRACTICE

PRACTICE

FINISH TRACING THE LETTERS OF EACH ROW
AS PROVIDED BY THE EXAMPLES!

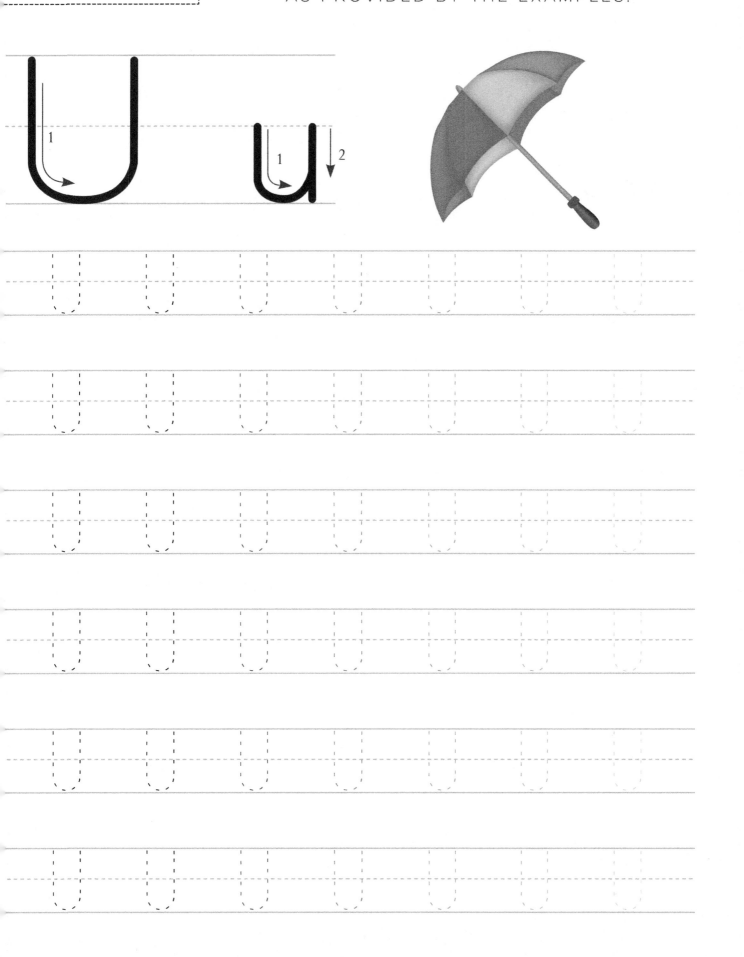

PRACTICE

FINISH TRACING THE LETTERS OF EACH ROW
AS PROVIDED BY THE EXAMPLES!

PRACTICE

FINISH TRACING THE LETTERS OF EACH ROW
AS PROVIDED BY THE EXAMPLES!

PRACTICE

FINISH TRACING THE LETTERS OF EACH ROW
AS PROVIDED BY THE EXAMPLES!

PRACTICE

PRACTICE

PRACTICE

FINISH TRACING THE LETTERS OF EACH ROW
AS PROVIDED BY THE EXAMPLES!

FINISH TRACING THE LETTERS OF EACH ROW
AS PROVIDED BY THE EXAMPLES!

FINISH TRACING THE LETTERS OF EACH ROW
AS PROVIDED BY THE EXAMPLES!

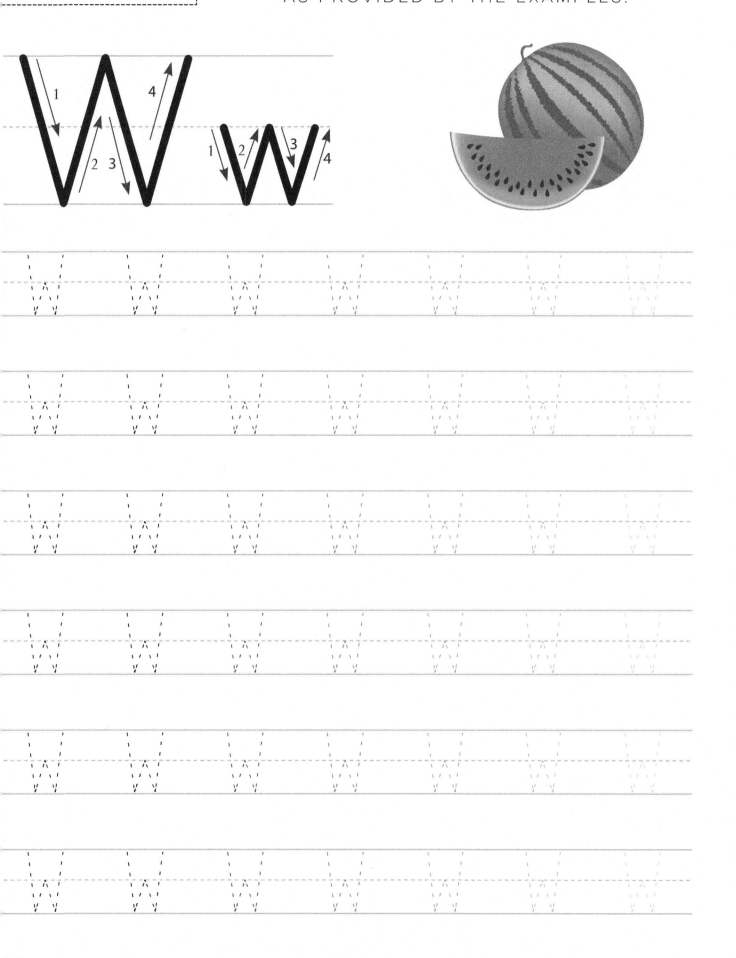

PRACTICE

FINISH TRACING THE LETTERS OF EACH ROW
AS PROVIDED BY THE EXAMPLES!

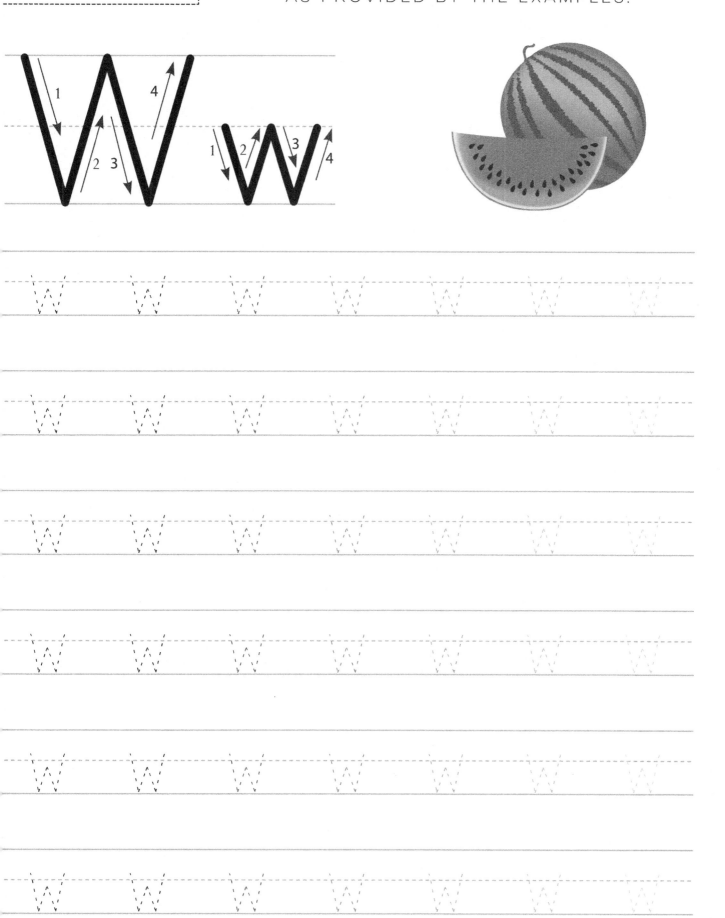

PRACTICE

FINISH TRACING THE LETTERS OF EACH ROW
AS PROVIDED BY THE EXAMPLES!

PRACTICE

FINISH TRACING THE LETTERS OF EACH ROW
AS PROVIDED BY THE EXAMPLES!

PRACTICE

FINISH TRACING THE LETTERS OF EACH ROW AS PROVIDED BY THE EXAMPLES!

PRACTICE

FINISH TRACING THE LETTERS OF EACH ROW
AS PROVIDED BY THE EXAMPLES!

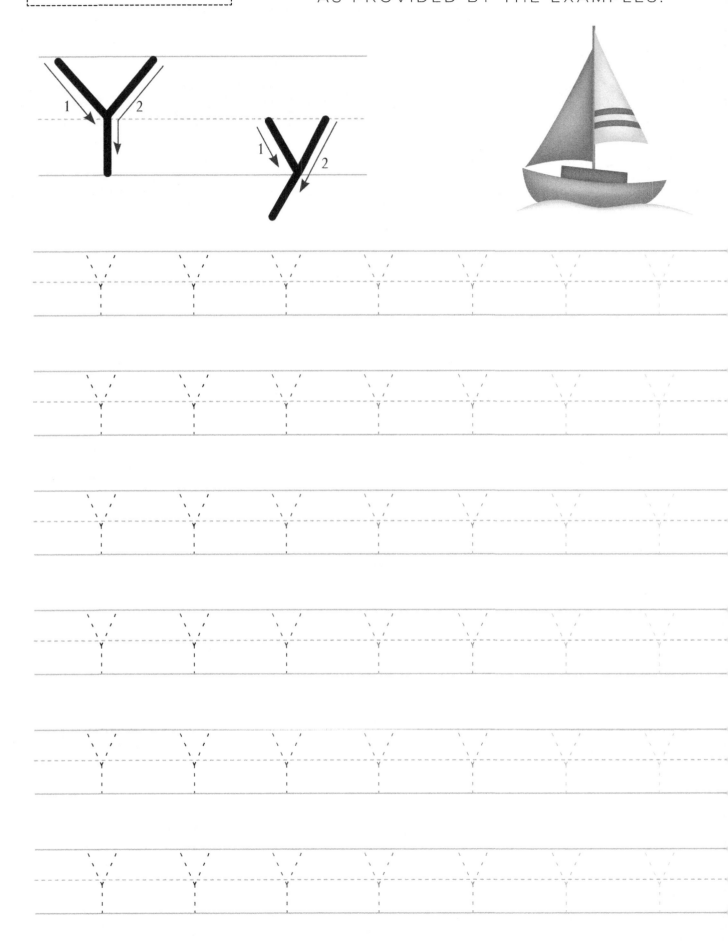

FINISH TRACING THE LETTERS OF EACH ROW
AS PROVIDED BY THE EXAMPLES!

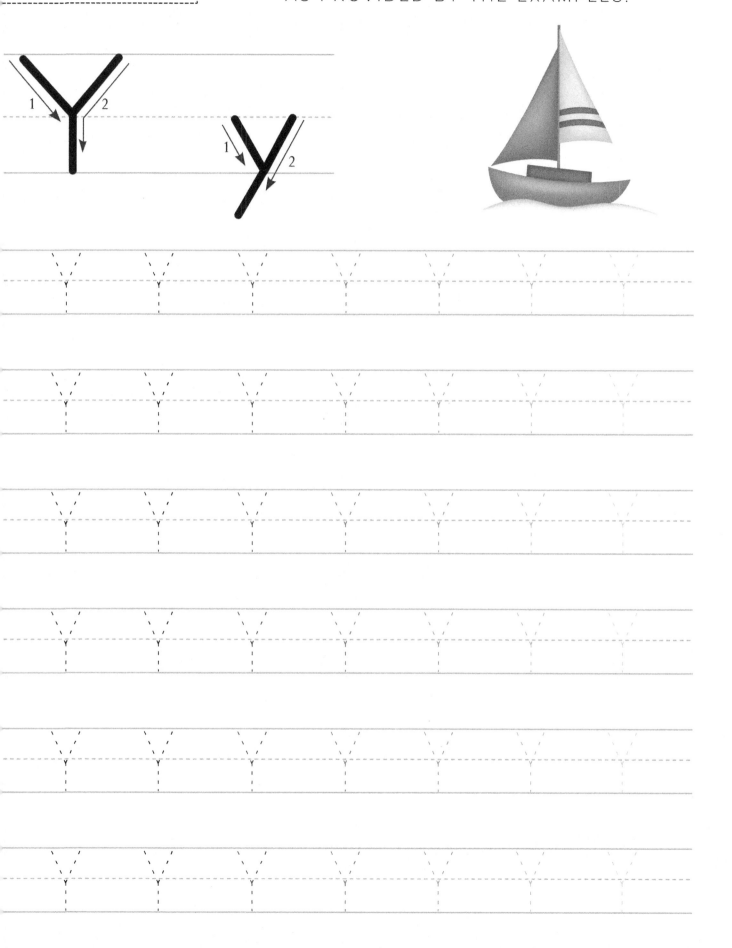

PRACTICE

FINISH TRACING THE LETTERS OF EACH ROW
AS PROVIDED BY THE EXAMPLES!

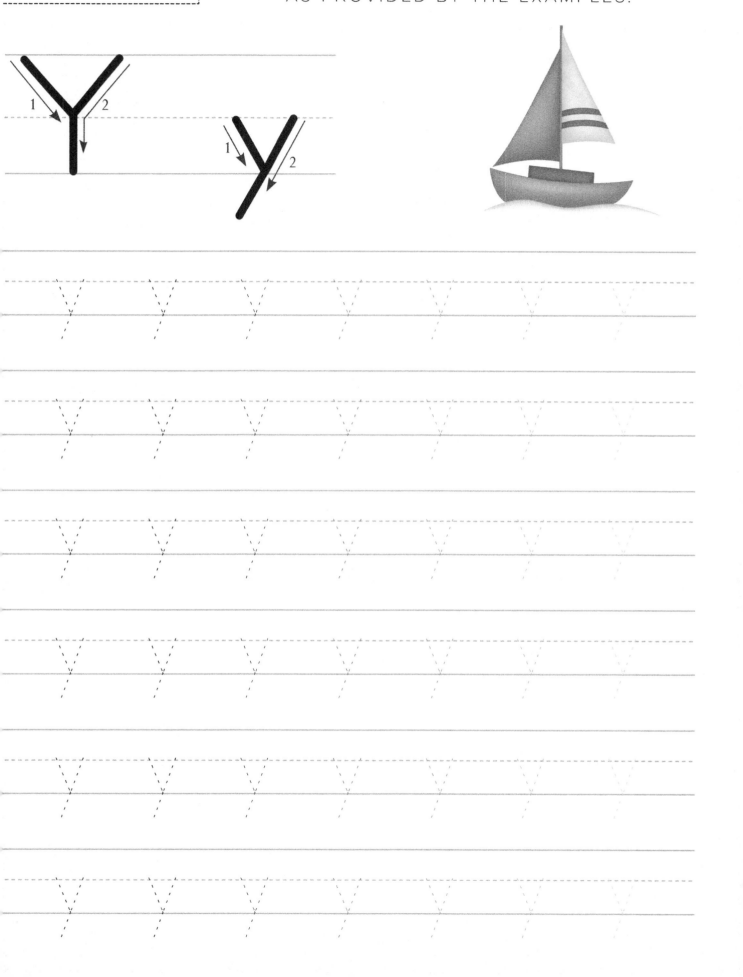

FINISH TRACING THE LETTERS OF EACH ROW
AS PROVIDED BY THE EXAMPLES!

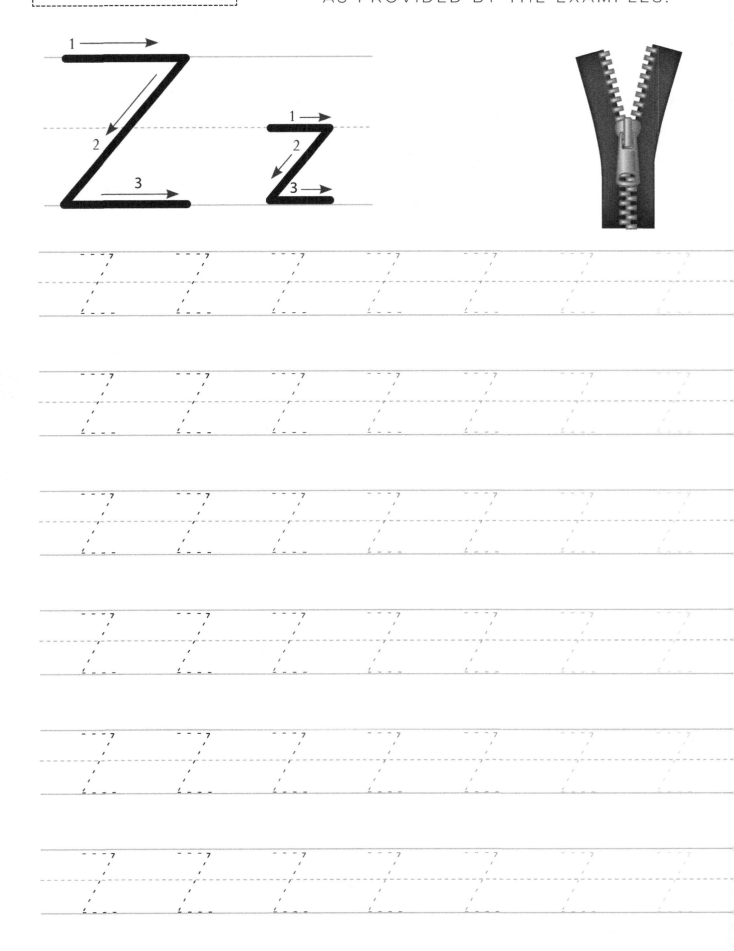

PRACTICE

FINISH TRACING THE LETTERS OF EACH ROW
AS PROVIDED BY THE EXAMPLES!

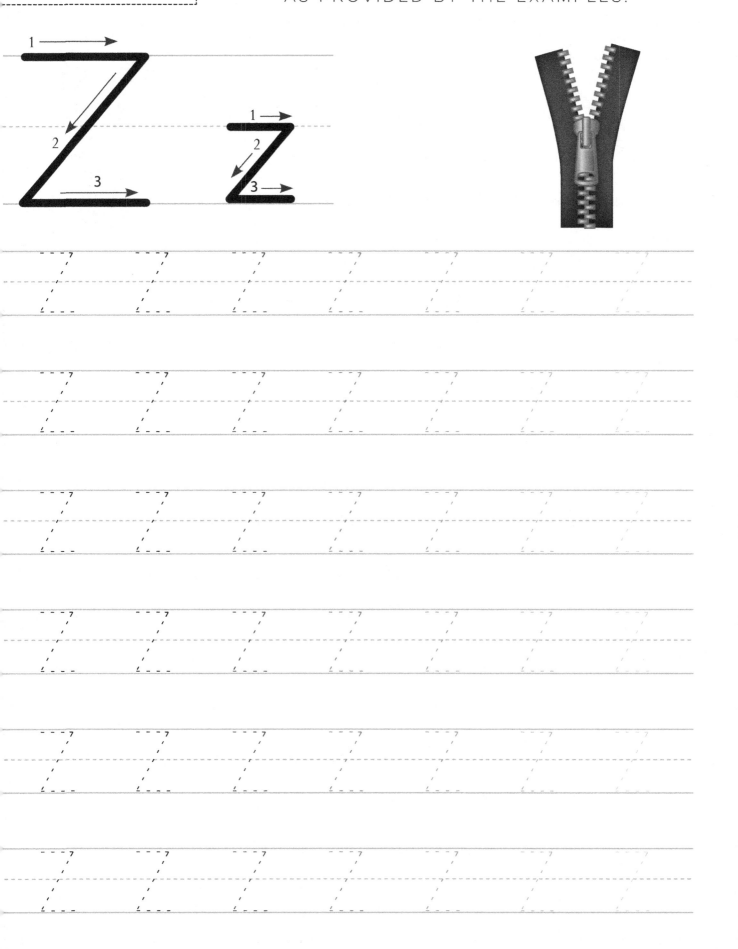

FINISH TRACING THE LETTERS OF EACH ROW
AS PROVIDED BY THE EXAMPLES!

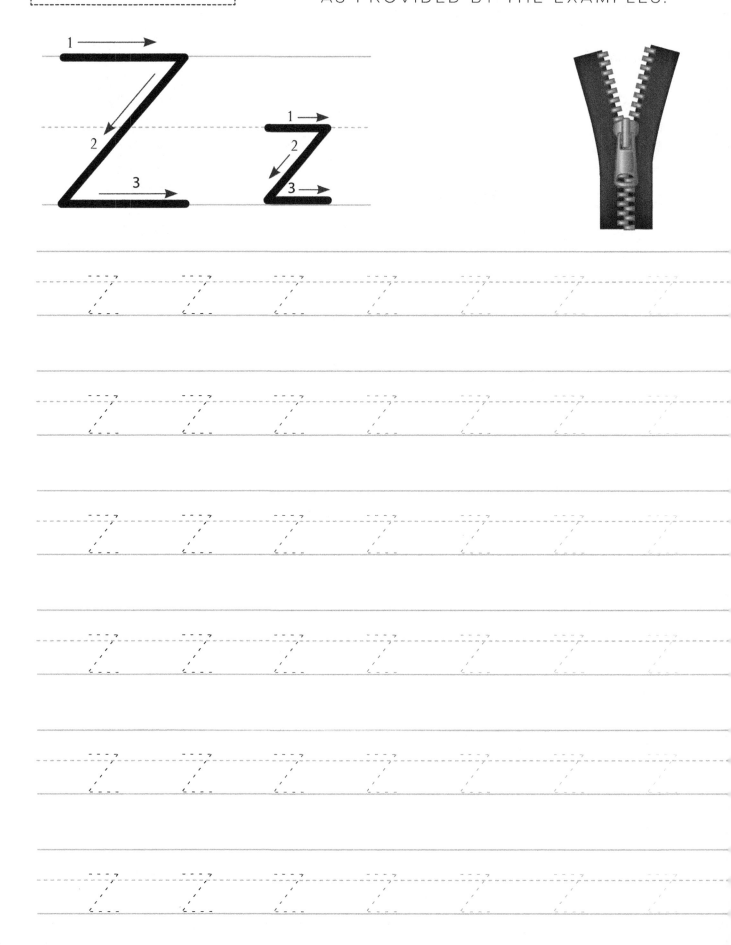

FINISH TRACING THE LETTERS OF EACH ROW
AS PROVIDED BY THE EXAMPLES!